Navigating the Seas of Human Connection

Dr. Larry J. Powitz

ISBN: 1503086690
ISBN 13: 9781503086692

ABOUT THE AUTHOR: LARRY J. POWITZ, ED.D

Dr. Powitz has had a 38 (plus) year career as a school psychologist, a clinical psychologist, a college professor and a psychologist intern supervisor. He is past president of The Chicago Association of School Psychologists and currently maintains a private practice in clinical psychology and psychotherapy. He has taught college level courses in Personal Growth Psychology and conducted seminars in group dynamics and interpersonal relations. He has come to know people around him by being a friend, a husband, a parent, a grandparent, a therapist, a lecturer, a public school teacher, a student, and a keen observer. He holds a master's degree in clinical psychology and a doctorate in educational and counseling psychology.

Dr. Larry (as he is often called) has always had a penchant for writing. He has published professional type articles but this is his first attempt at a book. We hope you find it meaningful and come back for more.

C: 03/25/2013
Larry J. Powitz, Ed.D.
Arlington Heights, IL. 60004

THE PROMISE

You will discover a brand new way to view and evaluate all your relationships and associations.

You will learn to recognize the very ingredients that make some human connections so rewarding and others so disheartening.

ACKNOWLEDGEMENTS

To my wife Bonnie, to my sons Jack and Paul, my daughter Diana and their spouses: Kimberly, Tiffany Clark and Tiffani Tolbert respectively for their encouragement and support.

A very special thanks to Paul Powitz for his guidance and time consuming assistance during the early phase of preparing the manuscript. And a great big THANK YOU to Tiffani Tolbert for the countless hours spent preparing the document for publication. And to Tiffani's mom, Beatrice Tolbert, for taking a special interest in the writing of this book. Her input was invaluable. And finally, thanks Curtis Caldwell for creating a unique piece of art that captures the essence of this book.

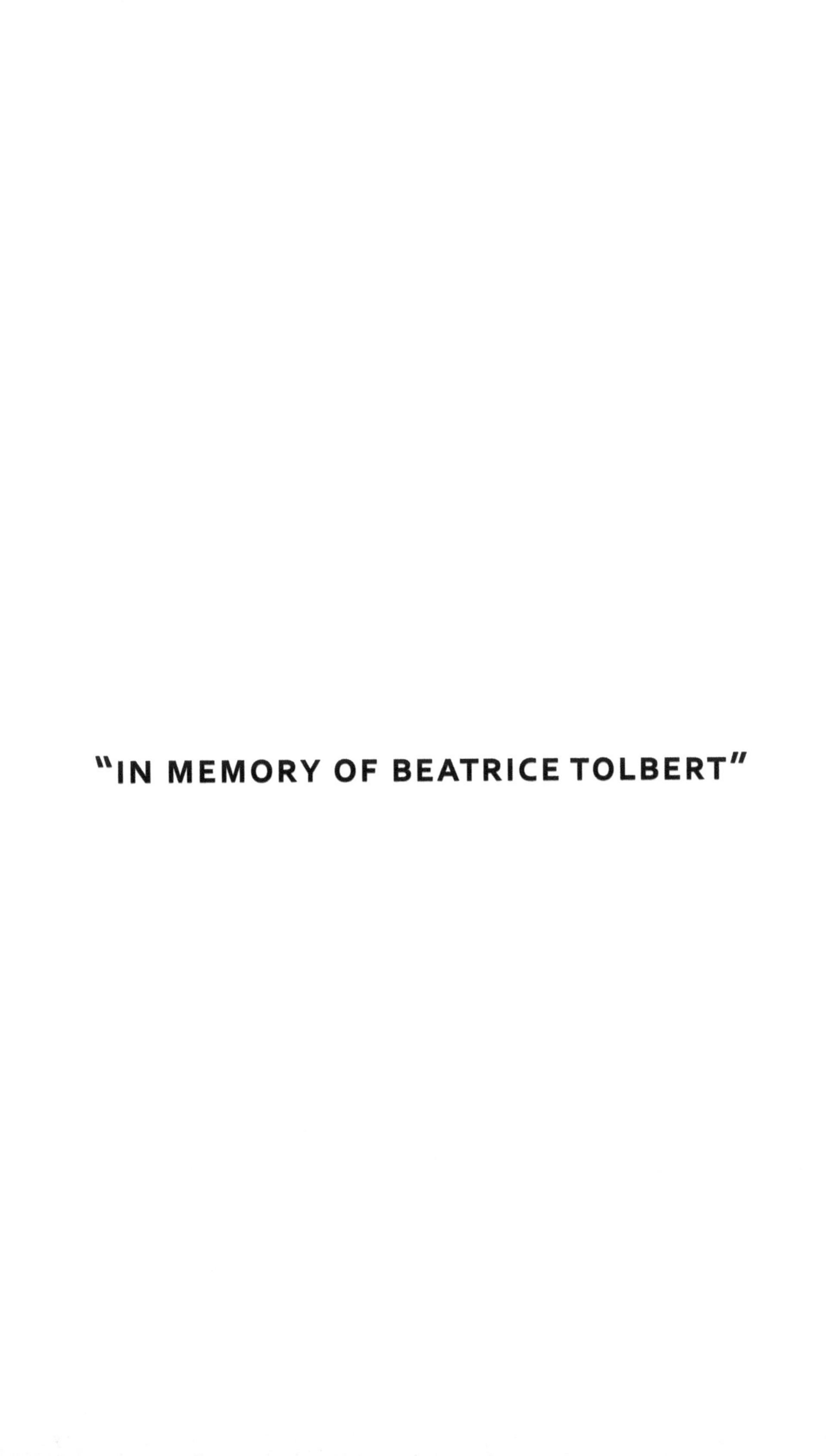

"IN MEMORY OF BEATRICE TOLBERT"

TABLE OF CONTENTS

Chapter 1

FOREWORD

(Preface)

Most of us would agree that relationships with significant and not so significant people in our lives can get quite complicated, confusing, and disheartening. But they can also bring you great joy and a sense of completeness and belonging. Wouldn't it be comforting if we could predict which ones will prove to be stable and fulfilling, which ones less than desirable, and which ones might be headed for disaster.

This book can help us predict what to expect from people who occupy places in our lives. It's basically a guide to promote interpersonal order and understanding as you travel through all your relationships and associations. I offer you a unique and entirely new way to look at your human connections. The book divides interpersonal relations into easy to understand categories and levels- each with its own descriptors and methods to help you analyze the status of your interpersonal world.

GIVE THIS BOOK A TRY.
IT WILL HELP YOU SORT THINGS OUT.
-Dr. Larry J. Powitz

Introduction

Popular, theoretical and empirical (research based) psychology have all studied the complexities and dynamics of interpersonal relationships. Books and publications devoted to interpersonal psychology are fascinating but often require an academic lifetime to digest.

In this book I offer an easy, clear and straight forward way to define and categorize human personal interaction and in the process reduce its complexities to an understandable and meaningful level. The categorizations to follow should help us understand, predict and evaluate where we are in many of our personal relationships (associations). They are presented as a guide by which to navigate and clarify your everyday involvement with significant persons in your life.

People frequently ask themselves questions that relate to the status of their interpersonal relationships and associations. Here are just a few questions I've heard along the way: "Is that person really a friend or just an opportunist; if she really loves and cares for me, why didn't she visit me when I was in the hospital; how come my adult daughter never talks to me about anything important; I thought we'd be friends for life-what the heck happened ; come to think of it I've never met my business associate's wife or kids-his personal life is a mystery; I still don't know why my brother is so angry with me-it's been 5 years since we've talked? (Or) I met this great gal on my flight from Boston to San Francisco and lost her at baggage claim-I can't stop thinking about her. Is that all there is?

Making sense out of our human connections or disconnections can get quite complicated, disheartening and even depressing as well as bring us great joy. What to expect from them, how not to be disappointed by certain outcomes and most importantly how simply to be at peace with the stature and quality of your interpersonal relationships is addressed in this book and so I present this guide to help you make sense out of all the potential complications that could arise as we interact with each other.

Please stick with it. Read it carefully and I am confident you will come away with a new understanding of how associations and relationships form, how they are defined, why they can be so unpredictable and finally how we can manage them.

Defining Characteristics of the Guide to Human Association

First this guide is intended to operate between **Two Adult Individuals** who have, at least, an association. You know them by name (faulty memory, notwithstanding); you can recognize them in a crowd, and know them well enough to carry on a conversation. A fleeting association may be an exception (see below).

The author chooses to define human association by degrees of intensity or involvement which may or may not be tantamount to what is commonly referred to as a relationship. In the present scheme you will see that acquaintances and fleeting associations (see below) do not reach the level of a relationship. Partial Association (see below) may or may not be equated with what is commonly termed a relationship. However, for purposes of continuity "association" and "relationship" may be used interchangeably.

This matrix of human involvement has as its center the interplay between two people (associates). Needless to say, this dynamic interplay can become quite complex especially when the partners view the importance or quality of the relationship or association "differently." Thus, the parties may be operating on two distinct levels and hard feelings may ensue when this "schism" is revealed. In other words in a particular association or relationship one might ask whether the feelings about each other are mutual or one-sided, i.e., "Are we both committed to each other or just me to you." Of course, harmony (reciprocity) is realized when both partners are contributing equally, i.e., showing equality of feelings, perspective and attitude so that the relationship has balance and power. The present scheme ideally presumes the individuals involved are in sync relative to the import and importance of the association, but nonetheless, it can be adapted to many contingencies of human connection or disconnection. To clarify further, let's say one member says, "I know I love you and I am confident you love me-right!?" The other member responds, "Hold on, I like you a lot but let's not push it, I'm not ready for all that love and commitment stuff etc. etc."!! In this case, there remains a serious disparity of intention, emotion, feeling and perspective. The present system of classifying interpersonal relationships into various stages or levels of involvement seeks to promote order and make sense out of how and why we interact with one another even in the presence of disparity and conflict. No doubt, we need to sort out why we are treated in certain ways by our "associates" and why we treat them the way we do, so that this system works even though the parties are on different levels. Of course, it is vital that both parties understand what level they are on and what level their partner is on and when, in fact, they are on the same level. But that understanding is not always easy to come by.

It is human nature that when we are treated in a way that is consistent with a certain interpersonal level (see categories below) we tend to respond in kind and so we treat others the way we are treated. Indeed, our reactions to significant others are very often dictated by their actions toward us. That is, when we are whipped we whip back; when we are loved we love back. Of course, when we love and get whipped in return---- not good either. This disparity in human association is all too frequent and problematic. In some negative instances a new level of understanding and kindness may be required to heal out- of - control negativity (see positive operators below). This brings us to the next point: These categories or levels of association are not intended to be absolute or discreet but rather dynamic in nature. So that movement **(M)** between or among levels can be expected depending on the desire and motivation of the partners. In this regard movement **(M)** is dictated by what I term operators **(O)** which cause a relationship to move to a higher or lower level.

Negative Operators
Fragmentation and Disruption:

These often occur together. So that when a "riff," an altercation, a severe affront, a hateful argument or an intolerable happening between the parties occurs, disruption ensues and the relationship becomes damaged, broken into pieces (fragmented). Most likely the association will move to a lower level or even cease to exist, at least for a time.

Positive Operators

These are operators which facilitate mending and healing of a relationship. We all know them but perhaps practice them too infrequently: Honest and open discussion, active listening, understanding the other person's point of view, acceptance, sincere apology, and the crown operator of them all, FORGIVENESS, may result in reconciliation. On occasion these operators may unfold even without intensive, didactic (2 way) conversations or heart to heart discussions. That is they may occur simply with behavior by both parties that is tender, sincere and consistent over time. Positive operators usually result in positive/upward movement.

This will all become crystal clear as the categories of human association are revealed.

Chapter 2

(OUTLINE AND OVERVIEW)

Levels of Association

The following will serve as an overview and an advanced organizer for categories (levels) of Human Association

I. Complete Association (CA)

Type A.

1). Long-term and deep commitment (typically for life).
2). Not appreciably affected by fragmentation and disruption.

Type B.

1). Long term and deep commitment (perhaps for life).
2). More affected by fragmentation and disruption with potential for an extended period of disassociation.

II. Limited Association (LA)

Type A- LA Negative

1). Not necessarily a long term or deep commitment
2). Frequent, motivated and desired contact and ongoing communication; however motivated and desired contact may be suspect depending on circumstance.
3). Obvious or hidden agendas and/or psychological manipulation which are intentional and make relationship conditional.
4). Subject to fragmentation and disruption.

Type B:

LA Negative Minus Desire: (Motivated and Frequent but not desired contact. M+F-D).

1). All the characteristics of LA Negative Type A but association is only engaged in to please a third party.
2). Thus, motivation + frequency minus desire.

Type C: Positive (LA Positive)

1). Not necessarily a long term or deep commitment
2). Frequent, motivated, and desired contact and communication (ongoing).
3). No hidden agendas; no premeditated secrets; relationship does not labor under psychological or emotional manipulation; a fulfilling association.
4). Subject to fragmentation and disruption.

Type D: LA Unknown

A once LA-Positive or LA-Negative association ceases without particular explanation.

Type E: Diminishing Association.

A once LA-Positive or LA-Negative association becomes less frequent with implied reduction in motivation and desire.

III. Partial Association (PA)

A). Determined by specific role person plays in one's life, i.e., professional, familial, proximity to individual (neighbor, etc.).
B). Restricted by nature of association.
C). Subject to fragmentation and disruption.
D). Continued or frequent contact
E). May be positive or negative

IV. Empty Association (EA)

Type A:

1). Fallen from a higher level of association.
2). The result of severe fragmentation and disruption.
3). Total or severe lack of communication.

Type B:

1). Long standing noxious or negative issues with very limited (infrequent) communication.
2). Motivation to communicate promoted by external forces.

V. Ancillary Associations

A). Acquaintances
B). Fleeting Associations
C). Cyber Associations

*note: Limited Negative Association is listed before Limited Positive for reasons of clarity and to facilitate understanding of Limited Positive Association.

Chapter 3

(DETAILED DESCRIPTIONS)

Categories of Associations

Complete Association:

Type A:

This constitutes the most intense level. It is characterized by unconditional and undying love and affection for another person. It is defined by total devotion and caring. This association is for life! Commitment to the other individual is permanent, unwavering and ideally unbreakable. This category of interpersonal involvement is not susceptible to extended fragmentation or disruption. A "riff", an altercation or negative episode in the association lasts a relatively short time (usually not more than a few days to at most a few weeks) and is always mended or reconciled. The association here is the strongest of them all. As one might predict, the loss of a person at this very high level of human connection is so-so difficult for they are truly a part of you! - Indeed the connection here is complete. Examples might be child/parent, siblings, spouses, and life partners, loyal and lasting friendships. It is a gift to be this close to another human being, to share their soul as it were.

Complete Association (CA):

Type B:

This level has all the ingredients of Type A except it is vulnerable to extended fragmentation and/or disruption. So that a negative altercation may result in a relatively long period of "disassociation" (i.e., perhaps months or even years). But sincere forgiveness, reconciliation and/or a new understanding typically happens and the relationship returns to a solid and healthy one with characteristics of Type A. It is important to note that in complete association-Type B, the basic feeling and emotion of a complete relationship never leaves the individual (s) and at some level may be compartmentalized during the period of "disassociation". Of course, there is always the unfortunate possibility that things may never be as they were. Where are those positive operators?

Limited Association (LA):

By its limited and conditional nature this level of association does not have the same quality of devotion, loyalty, caring and commitment as a complete association but it can be very meaningful, intense and endure for a long period, even a life time (LA Positive). At times it can even mimic a complete association (CA).

As with CA it reaches the level of a relationship. However, it can be an interesting and tricky type of human connection with definite negative and positive components as we shall see. And for purposes of clarity, it can be divided into five subtypes, A, B, C, D and E (Note: LA Negative is presented before LA Positive only for purposes of contrast and clarity and not because it is a higher level type of association).

Type A (Limited Association-Negative):

Type A is termed Limited Association (LA) Negative and is described as follows:

One might presume that one is in a LA Positive relationship but lo and behold the individual becomes aware that he/she is excluded from certain aspects of the other person's life and/or he/she is not allowed to talk about certain personal topics or areas of interest that one would expect to be privy to as in a LA Positive association. You might simply say in LA negative there are secrets. For example, "How come when you see those people (selected friends, certain family members, work associates etc.) I am never included, informed or even allowed to be in their presence. Why won't you discuss where you went on vacation and who you were with, etc. etc." In LA Negative at least one individual is aware of the exclusion, accepts it and approves of it. It may be the case that spouses, family members, "good" friends, siblings, romantic partners, a married man and his mistress, a married woman and her lover can all be involved in a LA negative association.

Remember, in LA Negative, there is typically real caring for the other person, real devotion but there are issues, sometimes unstated or buried that set up boundaries (limits) between the parties.

Sometimes you don't become aware of limitations until you are well into the relationship and certain restrictions can come as a surprise or even a shock. For example, social plans suddenly change because someone is going to be at a gathering that your partner does not want you to come in contact with so your invitation is revoked.

It could be that you-yourself have had a part in alienating certain people in your partner's life and as a result you are precluded from seeing them (and vice-versa-it works both ways). But same is not resolved. The point is no matter who is to blame you remain cutoff or precluded from important aspects of your partner's life.

Another scenario which fits in this category, although it is often not clear cut, is a situation wherein one partner has emotive power over the other partner. This disparity in the relationship may produce an imbalance in authority and power often resulting in victim and perpetrator. But it's tricky, for interpersonal transactions are often subtle and usually benefit the perpetrator. In disguised and manipulative fashion the quiet but effective abuser uses and gets his way with the naïve victim. In this situation the perpetrator plays on the good nature of his unassuming partner with deception underhandedness, hard to detect lies, hidden agendas, masterful control techniques, etc.

Perhaps to make my point allow me to ask if you have ever been in a relationship that was ongoing, that you were motivated to be in, and that you desired but eventually discovered was not in your best interests but only in the best interests of your partner? Did you ever feel like a pawn emotionally serving someone else's needs? It often takes time to catch on. You may even feel like you're in a LA Positive relationship. But, guess what, at times it just doesn't feel right. The interesting thing is the relationship continues for longer than a reasonable person might expect. This situation can also be termed LA Negative with all the components of frequency, motivation and desire despite the negative circumstances. It is important to add that this brand of LA Negative can be very hurtful and ultimately explosive.

Type B (Limited Association Negative-Minus Desire):

In this subtype of the LA negative category (termed LA-Negative Minus Desire) one or both partners are motivated to form the association or "relationship" only because they wish to please a third party. Unlike LA negative Type A, basic caring and devotion for the other person is basically absent. As you will see it may appear to be a partial association (see below) but the frequency (F) of the contact and the social engagement of the parties brings it to a higher level even though real desire to be with the person is absent. An example might be as follows: In accommodating to your spouse, you "hang-out" with your husband's best friend from high-school and see him more or less frequently to make your partner happy-he enjoys this guy. But you can't wait for him to leave!! Another example: You tolerate your best friend's husband because you really adore your best friend, etc. etc... Even here, there is a kind of hidden agenda. I might add that this brand of LA negative may acquire a bit of acting for a very long time. The result: Your association is not fully open and/or honest with an absence of desire (LA Negative Minus Desire or M + F- D); wherein M = motivation F = Frequency and D = Desire.

Another kind of LA Negative in which there is frequency of contact and motivation and desire to see the person (although both are suspect) is a situation where the individuals may have had a very cordial and positive association (LA Positive, see below) but on one unfortunate occasion one or both members say some awful thing or do something inexcusable to the other member, causing severe disruption in the relationship. Maybe for a time they don't talk, but circumstances put them together again. They resume their relationship; they forgive but one or both NEVER FORGETS. This can be deceptive, for if a person never emotionally forgets (neuro or physical memory, notwithstanding) real forgiveness is suspect. This situation may find its place somewhere between Type A and Type B----but it is certainly limited. Loosely related to limited association-negative are those individuals I term "Pattern People.

Be Aware of Patterns:

Here, we may have a situation wherein some people in your community of relationships might hurt you once, apologize and then do it all over again and again and again. The time between insults is of no consequence. Be aware of the insincere and disingenuous Pattern People. They can present as Limited Positives but when you least expect it, they do something cruel and socially damaging to you and / or your loved ones. You forgive or overlook their often subtle passive aggressive acts; time goes by and lo and behold they do it again. BEWARE the PATTERN PEOPLE.

Type C (Limited Association-Positive):

Limited associations can have negative aspects as just described or they can be relatively void of such negativity and be mostly pleasing and positive (i.e., no intentional instances of being left out, see above). But, nonetheless, by their nature (ergo by definition) they are not the total package as in a complete association. You may really like the person, know them a long time, never have had a single uncomfortable moment with them, completely enjoy their company but they are not totally a part of your inner life, your "soul" as in a complete association. You help them move into their new home, have them stay at your house during tough times and good times, there is never any intent to psychologically/emotionally manipulate them to serve your own needs, but the deep commitment and bond as in CA is not there.

Hey, most of your friends (your good buddies), people we date, family members we see often and desire to see often, good neighbors and individuals we have a relationship with fall in this category, aptly named LA positive.

It is important to note that, LA positive can be deceiving and not clear cut. That especially happens when conditions are put on the relationship that are not the fault or intention of either party (assuming balance in the association). For e.g., being precluded from certain aspects of your partner's life that he/she has no control over; not discussing certain personal topics simply because they're very hurtful to you or your friend and not because there is an intent to exclude or hide information from either of you; preferring that you not associate with certain of your partner's friends, family, etc. because people outside of your partner insist. However, your partner does not approve of same and is completely open and honest about it and seeks your consult and OK before this happens (admittedly this is tricky and may even define the state of your association).

Type D: (Limited Association-Unknown)

Finally, distance is not typically a factor in either limited associations or complete associations, especially in these days of instant-techno-communication. However, being a distance apart because of school, job, and life situation may prove to be a test of the relationship. As one example, let us present a situation, wherein, a good friend moves away, perhaps, from Chicago to Santa Monica, California. You have had a limited positive association with this person. But now you hardly hear from them, i.e., limited texting, limited e-mailing and in the past two years they have never invited you out to California. No altercation fragmentation or disruption has occurred-so where are we in terms of our present scheme? Are they hiding something? Is there a hidden agenda? Have we gone from limited positive to limited negative? Or is it just one of those things? You still like them and want to see them and you have no reason to believe they are discounting you.

Other related examples may be an old high school or college buddy or work associate that you were pretty close to (LA positive) and for no apparent reason you never see him/her anymore. No doubt, you still are fond of each other but the old relationship just isn't happening. They do not fit into an Empty Association (see below), so where do they fit? There really is not an ongoing association but there still is a positive feeling about them. Perhaps your lives have gone in different directions? But, nonetheless, you really look forward to seeing them at the next reunion. These life situations beg for a corollary to limited associations. Again, let's label this condition Limited Association-UNKNOWN (LA U) - Type D

Type E: (Limited Diminishing Association)

Closely related to LA Unknown is Diminishing Association -Type E. A once LA-Positive or LA-Negative Association wanes often with no discernible explanation. You see the person less and less. Maybe there's lack of desire, maybe not. Maybe now you only enjoy each other once in a while. Maybe the bedrock of motivation that was once there is gone or is a lot less. People may lose interest in old "friends". Common experiences in the present no longer exist. This category, however, does point up that true long-term associations are a rarity, i.e., those lucky people who never get tired of each other.

Further Things to Consider:

In concluding the discussion of CA and LA it should be pointed out that some of these associations develop as time and experience march on. So that meeting a new friend or romantic interest for the first time and finding the association rewarding may in fact be only the beginning of an LA positive or LA negative union. But even in the early stages, it still may loosely be termed LA positive or negative; however, because of its infancy, it may be more vulnerable to fragmentation and disruption etc. Likewise the bonding so strong in CA develops through time-and becomes more defined as a function of experience. As discussed above, CA, Type B may be more vulnerable to fragmentation and disruption (see above). So if you will, let's call an LA Positive or Negative relationship with an intimate or amorous component **LA-Romantic** and an early stage association **LA or CA-Infancy**.

A Cautionary Note:

The infancy of a relationship can present unique challenges. One may tend to rush into a new relationship with such gusto and eagerness that one forgets that one doesn't know the person all that well. Always gage where you're at in a new friendship, etc. Let the new union develop slowly and reasonably. Go beyond whatever neediness you may have. The expectations inherent in a new relationship with all its unknowns are certainly different than a solid long term association. In other words be careful, just as you would with a new born infant. "Such carefulness should also extend to a renewal of an old relationship that has been absent for a LONG time. In some ways the infancy rule applies there too. You be the judge."

Partial Association (PA):

PA is defined by people in our lives that assume or fulfill specific roles (often professional but not necessarily); For example your M.D, your accountant, your lawyer, stockbroker, dentist, teacher, your student, your boss, co-worker, postal carrier, friendly grocer, your neighbor, little league coach, your plumber, hairdresser, chiropractor, your psychologist, etc.. With regard to one's neighbor: Because of the proximity, you may have frequent and cordial contact with the person. But ask yourself, if they moved away would you ever see them again? The answer might determine whether or not your association might go beyond the partial category. By the way political opponents would also fit in this category.

As a related matter, members of your family (extended or even immediate) whom you see infrequently and whom you see only because of their relation to you may be included here. Examples would be cousins, aunts, uncles, and even unfortunately (in some cases), sisters, brothers, parents that you might only see at weddings, bar mitzvahs, anniversaries, family reunions, funerals, but with whom you have no meaningful or desired relationship. In this category may also be included ex-wives or ex-husbands whom you see because of their role as mother/father to your children.

It is true that we intend for partial associations to be positive, cordial and even helpful and most of the time if they are not they will cease. But sometimes they might continue out of necessity. You "hate" your boss, your coworker, your next door neighbor etc. you dislike the bedside manner of that physician but, hey, he is the best at what he does- so the association continues. And when it comes to the coworker in the next cubicle, you just do not like her but she is here to stay and you must get the job done. And your next door neighbor, well, you must grin and bear it for you have to face his surliness most every day----there he is when you take out the garbage, drive up your driveway or sprinkle your lawn.

Again, it is important to note that a PA can grow into a higher level association. But this may become complex when it involves a professional relationship. For example, it might not be ethical for a psychiatrist and the patient he treats to maintain a social relationship beyond the treatment setting.

Empty Association (EA):

Next, we have the sad but all too frequent associative state termed Empty Association. We must be careful here, however. Those unfortunate enough (although in some instances it might be a relief) to be caught in this negative-empty state have "fallen" from a previous level. Empty Association is divided into two types.

<u>Type A:</u>

By the process previously described of fragmentation and/or disruption one becomes completely disassociated from a person with whom they once had a relationship. But the altercation, disruption was so severe, so "unforgiving" that the parties stopped communication and the association terminates. It is consistent and logical that one may have fallen from a Complete Association, Type B (see above). In this case, the noxious event was so severe that chances for a return to CA, Type B may seem unlikely. But remember the scheme I present is dynamic, i.e., movement up or down is always possible, especially with CA, Type B. People experiencing empty associations may have been involved in CA Type B, LA, or PA. By definition, CA Type A is not susceptible to an Empty Association.

Recovery from the jolt of an EA is possible because of the M factor (movement up and down the categories/levels) and the all-important operators known as forgiveness, compromise, and acceptance. Of course one or both parties may choose to stay (even permanently) in EA. This bears further commentary. When all communication stops it is indeed a difficult situation. If one member wishes to reconcile and the other does not, balance (as noted earlier) is lost and the Empty state will continue and continue.

Type B:

It does happen in the course of daily life that one comes across an individual that you were once in a relationship with-but now are disassociated from. You may speak briefly; you may even email once or twice but there is no real push to reunite or move in a positive direction. Here an empty association does not necessarily involve a complete absence of communication but the engagement is VERY strained and purposely infrequent. Parties may talk to each other because circumstances dictate they "must" as in a contentious divorce, or in a family dynamic that has gone sour. Once again, parties "communicate" only because factors outside themselves depend on it, but in fact the individuals have "no use" for or are indifferent to one another and have no real relationship. In all of these situations the parties have fallen from a higher more positive association. Again, Empty Associations are difficult but they are a reality.

Cyber Association

The computer age with all its accessories, i.e., techno-devices (I phones, I-pads, I-pods, electronic note pads, smart phones with endless apps and not so smart phones, smart watches, droids, and super droids and devices whose robotic voice speak back to you, etc.) along with their bed follows, social networking, texting, emailing, skyping, tweeting, instant messaging, face -booking, etc., may as we speak be changing the landscape of human association or at least modifying it. Therefore, the dynamic of computer- techno communication as it affects basic interpersonal relatedness, as delineated in this text, deserves at least a mention.

How are levels of human associations (relationships) as described herein affected by internet communication i.e., often voiceless and void of real in person to person communication. Let's take an everyday example; there you are in cyber space, where you find yourself substituting print for the nuances and subtleties of message and personality inherent in the human voice. Beyond this, how often do we say exactly what we think in a text, email, on face book or twitter that we dare not "say" in real time face to face, live communication. And how often do we say what we mean, perhaps impulsively, and then are deleted as a face book friend or "unfriended"? (Is this tantamount to an Empty Association?) And how often does it happen that you're simply in a bad mood or haven't got enough sleep and you go on face book, for example, and don't intend to make "trouble" but your well-intended message comes out wrong. You could spend hours apologizing. Once in print, it's out there. The fact is that when we e-mail, etc. we are not privy to the nuances of facial expression or subtlety of human voice communication which might give us important feedback as to how we should conduct ourselves or in what spirit the message should be taken. And how often does this occur? : You are out to dinner with a good friend and they split their time between eye-contact with you and their beloved E-notebook, I phone, I pad or laptop. Or your immersed in conversation with this same friend, answering what you thought was an important question and notice as you are in mid - sentence that they are totally absorbed in internet gymnastics---- "Oh, sorry, what were you saying?"

The preceding, notwithstanding, cyber association is here to stay. It's more efficient, more expedient and more in tune with the rapid motion of the modern world, i.e., "I don't have time to talk; but I have time to text and get on my way".

And it can, at some level, keep people in frequent contact* with each other without the complication of actually having a "talking" conversation. ("I've never really spoken to you or actually seen you in person but I know all about you and your family---we're friends on face book.") In fact, cyber communication is becoming the cornerstone of business and social communication. But I ask again-how does all this new kind of "depersonalization" impact our established or budding associations. Again, consider an association, wherein, you have never physically met the person nor have never heard their humanity (their voice) live and in person.

In this regard, I ask does Skyping or video texting on occasion make up for communication dominated by a world wherein individuals "connect" via internet print-often void of seeing each other or hearing or listening to the spoken word. Does even seeing your friend's image and hearing his voice on a cyber-screen substitute for a handshake. Is social-networking really social?

And as an extreme example, how about that couple sitting across from each other in the corner booth at restaurant X and texting as opposed to actually facing each other and speaking.

*An important addendum to "frequent contact" is too much "frequent contact". Super technology has made us so easy to reach no matter where we are or what we're doing. Sometimes this is a good thing but at times "reachability" can be intrusive. It doesn't give us one moment to detach. To be in our "own ZONE" for a precious second (plus), what effect does too much connection have on our relationships?

Closely related to all this is a relative new phenomenon termed ONLINE DATING. Whether it's a particular service you subscribe to or whether you find yourself out there by yourself, be aware of the unknowns. Even if you have your potential partner's picture, even if they tell you all about themselves, even if you're taken in by their sexy, soothing and/or inviting voice---are they really who they say they are? Despite looking good, are they real or merely a cyber-creation. Be careful what you tell them. There is a "new thing" out there called MEETING THE PERSON in real life! Don't let loneliness make you vulnerable to deception. It could be the case that a Limited-Positive (romantic) relationship or even a Complete B relationship involving your spouse may be headed to some level of fragmentation or disruption. You enter an internet chat room. You strike up a "connection "with Mr. or Mrs. Charming and they seem to fill your immediate emptiness. This blind cyber association could play on your vulnerability and prevent you from working on real life relationships before you. Just be careful and think cogently about what you're doing.

And then there is the very sad situation of cyber bullying or toying with vulnerable people via the internet. As news reports or personal experience tell us such occurrences can end in tragedy. A group of hateful individuals get together and through the internet ridicule one weak person who becomes trapped in believing horrible lies about themselves. "Oh my G'd, it must be true; it's all over the internet. All my friends think terrible things about me. And here I sit ALL ALONE staring at this glaring screen. Why won't these evil words about me STOP?" Words on a potential victim's PC if authored by the wrong person can be so, so damaging and even lead to self-destructive behaviors. Are we talking here about a form of CYBER CRIME?

Another issue is the matter of depersonalization caused by the internet and all of its techno cousins. Examples of this depersonalization are many: I frequently hear people say, "I have 123 friends on face book; I have 150 friends; I have 200 friends." I ask what kind of "friends" are these? Where do they fit into the present scheme? Most recently I read an article in USA Today Magazine (09/2012) whose main intent was to point out how important and how healthy it is for sedentary people to start moving. As one means to this end they advocated the following: Instead of emailing your office buddies down the hall; get up and deliver the message personally. It'll get you moving and "won't kill valuable face time". Face time---indeed, a new term for the 21st century. Are we now in a race i.e., Cyber Contact vs. Communicating Live with a Real Person.? Is Face Time, having been around since Java Man, going out of style?

Nonetheless, many would say social networking via the internet, text messaging, on-line dating, emailing, tweeting, and face booking, etc., really enhances interpersonal communication and relatedness. It exposes individuals to all kinds of people with whom they would never have communicated and helps maintain established relationships. And, of course one must not be paranoid. There are a lots of good and decent people out there just waiting to "talk" to other good and decent people. Just be aware of the NO-GOODERS.

Oh well, perhaps passage of time, assisted by future, well designed studies will give us some answers as to how cyber association and even cyber "relationships" fit into the scheme presented in this book. As of now, we must leave it as an open issue.

One more thing: It is the case that a cyber-association begins or is established qualitatively much differently than a real life, in person meeting with a future friend, etc. Again, what this means for New Age human connection remains to be seen.

BEHOLD THE TECHNO-CONVERSATIONALIST

Perhaps, only tangentially related to this discussion is the emergence of the newly anointed computer knowledgeable individual. Some of these people are amazing. And they can be as young as a 5 year old kindergartener or as sophisticated as an adult whose expertise relative to every techno-device monopolizes every conversation. The flip side are those otherwise educated individuals who simply are computer ignorant or don't care about I-phones, or I- pads, etc. or simply choose not to partake in the cyber revolution. The interesting phenomenon is that these people who may be sitting at your dinner table with numerous graduate degrees may be entirely left out of the conversation when it turns to----" Let me tell you about my fantastic app. or my state of the art droid" ; or my Apple I-197. Oh, by the way, that interesting question you bring up, no need to discuss---let me access the internet and find the answer." It's almost as if one's accumulated knowledge is being usurped by computer talk or "machine "generated instant information. Sometimes I wonder where we fit in if we don't talk computers.

Ancillary Associations:

Acquaintances:

These associations (not really relationships) are more stable than Fleeting associations (see below) but they are relatively minor in the order of things. Without sounding condescending, they fill in the gaps within the totality of our interpersonal world but lack the human connection and investment that the others command (i.e., CA and LA and even PA)

Fleeting Associations:

A few examples might suffice: You are sitting next to an amenable individual on your flight from New York to Los Angeles. You digest their life story and never see them again-a fleeting association. They come; they go; but never stick. They may have made an impression but like the wind and what it gathers, away they go. You volunteer at a soup kitchen and have a soulful conversation with a homeless gentleman but never encounter him again. As meaningful as this may be, it is fleeting.

However, it is important to note that in some circumstances a fleeting association can be more than a "slam-bam-thank you ma'am". Indeed, it might last for days or even weeks; but it is discreet with a defined beginning and end. For example, you're on vacation and you and your travel companion meet another couple on an extended river cruise. The four of you get along famously for the whole two week period. The cruise ends; email addresses and phone numbers are exchanged. And you never hear from them or see them again and vice versa. A somewhat extended and positive association but fleeting, nevertheless. Do you see why this situation is not LA-Unknown? The experience was circumscribed. It was for a 2 week period that began and ended in a relative flash, high and mighty talk, notwithstanding. There was no long term relationship that broke apart. Remember in a fleeting association you do know the person but not for long. A fleeting association is separated from a partial association because the former is so short-lived.

Chapter 4

CONCLUSION: (RECAPITULATION)

And so there you have 5 main levels of human association and their subcategories with all attending complexities.

Think of people you know, people important to you, people you like, love and people on whom you can always rely. Then think of people you no longer associate with, no longer like/love and no longer depend on and finally people you never liked. Where do you and they fit into this scheme? Does this way of looking at interpersonal relationships help you sort out what to expect from others and yourself, help you clarify the place or role "significant" people play in your life? As you answer this question, remember that all relationship (associative) categories described and the totality of the entire scheme is dynamic, subject to movement and change and subject to both negative and positive directionality.

I am confident that the scheme presented will help you navigate through many of your associations (relationships). It should provide you with a kind of gauge to assist you in determining the quality and level of your connection to a particular person in question. Is that person really a friend, a good friend, a limited positive for example, a lesser association or someone you chat with in cyber space?

Sometimes not knowing or having a sense for what type of association you are in can be quite disconcerting. For instance, you might begin an association with someone and they act as if they were your best buddy. You rely on their "helpfulness, good nature, and accessibility", but soon something snaps and they begin to be uncomfortable with how close or intrusive the "friendship" or perhaps "romance" has become and set up barriers, disappoint you, cause you major inconvenience, and/or discount or manipulate you in some way. Because initially you did not gauge the association accurately, you kick yourself and say the perennial, "I should have known better"!

A Word to the Wise:

Be careful (but not paranoid) with new associations; being reasonably cautious and sensible without spoiling the good times should do. Remember, a new limited positive or limited negative can be very different from an established Limited Association (and even then things can be unpredictable). And a Partial Association mistaken for the more involved connection , LA Positive (+) for example, can also be troublesome.

Further, if one has the experience of moving down the associative scale and in some instances moving into an empty association, same can be quite disturbing, anxiety provoking or (the flip-side) very depressing and worse. The point is, I don't present these categories or movement, therein, lightly. Of course, movement can be positive and joyful, can involve real understanding and true forgiveness or, unfortunately, may involve strong negative feelings, broken promises and even throw one into emotional shock. I believe the latter can be avoided if you are smart about your relationships, and know what to expect. The present scheme should help. But it requires practice, without overdoing it.

Finally, it is important to note that I do not at this writing pretend to offer you a specific way to mend or heal your associations (relationships) or offer you detailed strategies on how to apply those positive operators (see above).

How and when to listen, understand the other person's point of view, accept, forgive and even reject the myriad of interpersonal offerings and communications, whether positive or negative, are basic to social skill development we hopefully learn as we live our lives.

Can someone like me or others help you (an adult) enhance or develop these skills? Lots of self-help books are out there and lots of professionals have tried. For that matter, when was the last time you offered advice to a troubled friend. What to do about bad-news associations is a whole other topic. For now let's classify, recognize and understand them. In this regard, **I can't emphasize enough the importance of accurately recognizing the category, level or status of the relationship of which you are a part.** For example, if things take a turn for the worse in your relationship with another, it is vital that you stop and ask yourself, "Before things got bad, what was the state of our connection, i.e., CA Type A; LA Positive/Negative; PA, etc." The ability to identify the level and quality of your relationship before the disruption and fragmentation should help you plan a course of action to deal with the interpersonal dilemma. For instance if you are in a Limited Association - Negative relationship should you have anticipated or expected this type of disturbance, in other words, "I'm not surprised ". But, if you're in a solid Complete Association Type A, this kind of "mess" may be totally unexpected. Therefore, you may invest a lot to fix the situation. The point is that recognizing the state of your interpersonal connection with significant people in your life should help you view your associations fairly, with understanding and sensitivity. And so as the title of this book suggests, let us embark on a voyage of discovery, a voyage which will give us new insight into the meaning and value of our relationships and associations. The waters of interpersonal relations can get pretty rough-you might even experience a storm or two. But understanding the people in your life, their motivation and agendas should help you navigate to calmer waters and hopefully to the safety of a secure port.

Most of all I wish for you calm seas and quiet air.

Chapter 5

LET'S PRACTICE – CASE SCENARIOS

OK----The scheme has been digested and now-----LET'S PRACTICE.

Presented below are 12 main case scenarios and at the end one very special case. Read each carefully and see if you can identify the relationship/associative status of each according to the levels of association I presented. Answers according to the author (me) are listed in the appendix. No Peeking Please. I hope we agree. Remember in some instances the two actors may be at different levels which certainly isn't ideal. If this is the case the scenario and question will clarify the situation.

CASE 1 (Karen and Bob)

Karen and Bob had been dating exclusively for almost a year. Things were going along pretty smoothly and they were very fond of each other. They had no secrets from one another and his friends were her friends and vice versa.

A). One might say they were at the level of________________

As the world turns, one day the subject of marriage came up. Bob exclaimed, "Oh no, I'm definitely not ready for that but I do love you". Karen countered, "I'm 34 years old; I want children; it's now or never". After some very nasty interchanges they had a bad break-up. They never spoke again.

B). Their status is______________

Case 2 (Abraham and Isaac)

Abe and Isaac are brothers. Abe is only one year older than Isaac but would never include his brother in any activities that involved his friends. To this day, although they see each other frequently and although as adults they do enjoy each other's company, they both don't know a lot about each other's comings and goings. In fact, when Abe is with one particular friend, Carl, Isaac is never invited to be around.

A). Based on the preceding, their relationship status is________.

To continue in the lives of Abraham and Isaac: On one occasion Abe threw a terrific party, with live music, balloons, food, games and prizes. Lots of family and friends were invited including CARL. Needless to say no invitation was issued to Isaac. Isaac, sick of being excluded, showed up anyway with his wife and kids, no less, and a very uncomfortable confrontation broke out between the brothers. Cruel words and threats were exchanged between Abraham and Isaac. Isaac left with his family and the party was not so terrific anymore. After things cooled down, the brothers resumed seeing each other but only because their mother insisted. Mom's happiness trumped their differences.

B). The level they are now operating on is______________.

Case 3 (Joan and Kathy)

Joan and Kathy, now adults, have been close friends since kindergarten. They are an integral part of each other's lives. They roomed together in college and their families are one BIG family. They have never had a quarrel that kept them apart for more than a few days--tops. Their deep caring and devotion to one another is obvious to all that know them. They possess the gift of lasting friendship.

A). The status of this relationship is____________________.

Time marches on and Joan and Kathy are well into their fifties. Kathy's husband loans Joan's husband a sizable amount of money that is never repaid. This causes a severe disruption between these once good friends. And so they stopped seeing and talking to each other for almost a year.

B). At this juncture their relationship (or lack of it) can best be characterized as____________________

Eventually despite the rift between the spouses, they renew their lost friendship and all things are as of old. They adore each other as much as ever, no secrets, no agenda, and complete devotion.

C). their new relationship status is now____________________.

Case 4 (Joe and Mr. Bean)

Mr. Bean is Joe's lawyer and tax accountant. Joe raves about his competency. "Mr. Bean (first name Jeffery) is the smartest guy I know." Joe only sees Mr. B. for legal and business matters.

A). their status is____________________

One sunny July 4th Joe had a barbeque, invited a few neighbors and Mr. Jeffery Bean. (Jeffery was friends with one of Joe's neighborhood buddies.) Joe discovered a side of Mr. Bean he never knew existed. This guy was not only a genius for detail; he was also fun and even funny. Joe and Jeffery became good friends beyond their professional association. They were always open and honest with each other, played golf almost every Sunday and confided in each other.

B). their new status is__________________

Case 5 (Lynda and Elizabeth)

Lynda and Elizabeth had never met in person. They got to know one another initially through an internet chat room. Lynda lived in Denver, Colorado and Elizabeth in New York City. Lots of details about their lives were shared but Lynda would never talk about her pre-teen years as if she were ashamed or hiding something. They both enjoyed their communications via the internet that went on for about 6 months before they decided to meet.

A). Before they met in person the status of their "connection" could be described as primarily_____________._If you could add a secondary more traditional category of association, what would it be?________________.

Eventually they met in person and for one year they spent all vacations together, many weekends and were intimate. After a time Lynn started to distance herself, traveled less to see Liz and told Liz finally, "It's best that we just stay friends and maybe when I get a chance I'll go east and see you---maybe." Liz was devastated; she thought that she had found her life partner, a person that was and would be a permanent part of her life. She was even planning to move to Colorado.

B). What kind of a relationship did Elizabeth hope for in terms of our scheme?
C). What is the status of the relationship as Lynda views it?_______________.

(Note: This scenario is complex with Lynda perhaps vacillating between 2 associative/relationship levels. Again it is always tough when individuals are in two different places. The adjustment is usually more difficult for the party who sees the relationship at a more positive level. (See answers and discussion in this Appendix below).

Case 6 (Christine and Thomas)

Christine always had a tough time in relationships with men. At 40 years of age she was divorced twice. Lo and behold at age 43 she fell in love with an older man, Thomas, 20 years her senior. Tom was a very wealthy gentleman, still married but estranged from his wife -sort of, i.e., twice a year on Christmas and Easter he would get together with his wife and children to celebrate the respective holidays. Christine was devoted to Tom and seemingly him to her. Tom would often say, "Chris is the best lover any man could have". But he would never let her meet his children nor certain of his good friends that knew his wife. There was even talk that he had another girlfriend and a child by her and eventually he admitted same. Countless times he would tell Chris that they were more important than her. But she put up with it. Nonetheless, the whole situation proved to be very tormenting for Christine.

A). Ok, at this juncture classify their relationship according to the present scheme____________________

Tom's and Chris' relationship despite periods of fragmentation and disruption lasted for 12 years. He financially supported her, bought her gifts and things and in return she did a whole lot for him including helping him almost every day in his import-export business and tending to his needs as he aged. One day without warning he said it's over, cut off all her goodies and support and never saw or spoke to her again.

B). And so the sad state of this association is ___________

Case 7 (Bruce, Barbara, and Parents)

Bruce was close to his parents all his life, as pure and honest and as caring as the gift of love itself. They never had an ongoing argument that lasted more than a few days.

A) The level they had been operating on is_______________.

As fate would have it Bruce, age 29, met Barbara, age 25, and an engagement and wedding soon followed. One big problem, Barbara and Bruce's parents, to put it softly, never liked each other. After the wedding, negative feelings exploded with much vigor. Bruce's dad insulted Barbara; Barb returned the fire and then demanded, "It's either me or those people". Result: Bruce didn't talk to his parents for almost a year.

B). The relationship status between Bruce and his parents is now_______________________.

After one year there was a meaningful and loving reconciliation between Bruce, mom and dad and things were once again civil but not quite as complete as they once were. He saw his parents frequently and cared about them but the comings and goings of his wife and her family were kept from Bruce's mom and dad; Bruce really didn't like the situation. But he wanted peace.

Barbara's "relationship" with her husband's parents was unfortunately another story. She only saw them very infrequently with Bruce and only had contact with them to please her husband. Bruce's parents felt the same way. Sadly! Those positive operators discussed in the text never came into play.

Ok---This scenario presents three inquiries:

1). In light of the heartfelt mending, Bruce and his parents are now at level______________________________.
2). Barbara's relationship with Bruce's parents is at______ __________________________.
3). And if we can assume that Bruce and Barb (despite all that has gone on) are very much in love and are devoted to each other for life, then their level of association is__________________________.

Case 8

You frequent a certain store where you buy most of your clothes. You especially trust a certain sales associate to select all of your garments for special occasions. This person has been waiting on you for years and you trust their expertise and taste implicitly.

This association is______________.

Case 9

It is late at night; you are far from home. You stop at a popular but unfamiliar supermarket and drugstore. You wander through the store to find a certain brand of cough syrup. You're lost in a maze. Where is the pharmacy section? A kind woman customer asks if she can help you look for something. You respond, "Oh please, where is the pharmacy, cough medicine etc... Hack, Hack." You begin a conversation with her as you walk across the store to the shelves with products for a cold/cough. You really enjoy your time with this pleasant woman. You say thanks, and say good-bye (forever).

This level is__________________

Case 10 (Carl and Tony)

Tony and Carl started out as really good work buddies. After time they became best friends. Then Carl's wife needed to be near her parents and they moved to another state. Tony and Carl communicated for a while but after a time the emails etc. became infrequent and all connection just stopped. Never a harsh word between them. In terms of our levels of human connection, where do Carl and Tony fit?

This Level is____________________

Case 11 (Sophia and Roberta)

1). Sophia and Roberta are roommates. They get along great, study together have been to each other homes and are friends. Roberta is much prettier than Sophia. Sophia likes this certain fellow and never wants to double date with Roberta and her guy. In fact Sophia never invites Roberta to co-ed social gatherings she organizes. Roberta, despite her good looks is not as popular as Sophia, but accepts things as they are, at least for now.

The best descriptor for this scenario is Level_______________.

2). As the semester rolls on, Sophia out does herself and throws a Big party at the college union hall. Roberta is not invited. Roberta has had enough. She goes anyway with a date. For all to see, she confronts Sophia, gets in her face and says, "How does it feel to be the ugliest girl at this so-called Party!!!! Sophia starts to cry and in between tears tells her roommate to GET OUT and take her freaky date with her.

Needless to say they were no longer roommates and went into an Empty Association (Type A) mode.

However, in their senior year they became friends again and the friendship didn't stop with graduation. They saw each other frequently with boyfriends and without boyfriends.

One day they were out alone together and Sophia said to Roberta, "I'm so sorry, I left you out when there were boys around. I was jealous of how you looked, please forgive me." Roberta responded, "I do forgive you. But I will never forget."

Sophia replied, "Roberta, remember you called me 'Ugly' in front of all those people. I know you didn't mean it. I might have deserved it. On second thought, let's both really forget all about it."

Ok, where are these 2 former roommates in terms of relationship status?

Case #12 (Charlie and Claudia)

Charlie thought, after reading "Navigating the Seas of Human Connection", that he was in a Complete Association Type A with his true love Claudia. They moved in together exactly 2 years ago---kind of an anniversary. On this anniversary day Claudia, over morning coffee, says with a most serious look, "Charles, I don't know what I want---I just don't think you're the one, maybe". She moves out, goes to live with her girlfriend but leaves most of her things behind. Although Charlie is devastated, Claudia and he continue to communicate. Charles thinks he can work things out; Claudia is not so sure. Months go by and Claudia is still living with her friend. They're still talking and seeing each other at least once a week. Charlie is confused.

Charles' feelings, notwithstanding, objectively what is the level of their association at the moment? ______________

CASE # 13 (a special life style)

Ronald never had a lot of friends growing up and even now, except for people he knows on the job, really doesn't "hang-out" with anyone. Ronnie lives alone, never married, no children and his extended family (mom, dad, sister, etc.) are simply not in his life. He is 45 years old and has had the same job as a computer tech. for 20 years. Ronnie is a loner and always has been. He prefers it that way. He's not depressed or forlorn or in need of extensive psychotherapy; he's just Ronnie. His associations are basically acquaintances or of the fleeting or partial association type (fellow employees at work). To the outside observer Ronald may seem like a "Lonely Guy "(like the movie with Steve Martin) but he does not consider himself lonely, just alone. Relationship categories just don't pertain to him. He eats alone, goes to the movies alone, has a party of one when he plays golf and when he watches TV he is completely in charge of the remote. Who knows what the future will bring? However, as of this moment, Ronald can best be described as THE HAPPY SELF-CONTAINED MAN.

Maybe it's best not to formally fit Ronnie into any relationship categories----let's just let him be. Certainly, there are as many scenarios out there as there are people. Good luck in applying Our Scheme.

May it help you understand yourself and the people you choose to let into your life!!!

C: 03/25/2013. Dr. Larry J. Powitz

Appendix: Answer Key To Let's Practice:

CASE I

A.) LA positive (romantic)
B.) Empty Association, Type A

CASE 2

A.) LA Negative
B.) LA Negative minus Desire or motivation + frequency- desire

CASE 3

A.) Complete Association. Type A
B.) Empty Association. Type A
C.) Complete Association. Type B

CASE 4

A.) Partial Association
B.) LA Positive

CASE 5

A.) Cyber Association; LA Negative
B.) Complete Association A
C.) The author's view: A once LA Negative Association transitioning into a LA diminishing association, Type E with a not so very bright future. (Remember this is Lynda's view.)

CASE 6

A.) LA Negative with complex manipulation and romantic encounters. Who was the prime manipulator? You decide.
B.) Empty Association, Type A

CASE 7

A.) Complete Association, Type A
B.) Empty Association, Type A
3 inquires:
1.) Limited Association-Negative but loving. (Note: the inclination is to label CA, Type B-but read it carefully)
2.) Empty Association, Type B (Note: This would assume, for. example, that Barbara and Bruce's parents were once at the level of Limited Association minus desire, i.e., M+F-D. Please reread pg.15 carefully)
3.) Complete Association, Type A

CASE 8

A Partial Association

CASE 9

A Fleeting Association

CASE 10

Limited Association Unknown, Type D

CASE 11

1.) Limited Negative;
2.) Limited Positive (but perhaps tentative; time will tell)

Case 12

Limited Association Type E (Poor Charlie-- He thought he had a Complete A relationship. But his partner, well you saw what happened. His only hope---maybe someday a Complete B with dear Claudia.) Catching on to how it takes TWO. The scheme does have its twists and turns.

Well, congratulations---you're at the helm of the interpersonal relation---SHIP. You are ready to write your own captain's log. One might start by listing selected people you know (significant in your life or otherwise) and identify them by the scheme presented. This just might give you a new, interesting and meaningful way to view and manage your social world.

Larry J. Powitz, Ed.D
Arlington Heights, IL. 60004
C: 03/25/2013

www.ingramcontent.com/pod-product-compliance
Lightning Source LLC
Chambersburg PA
CBHW030532290526
45786CB00004B/1701

* 9 7 8 1 5 0 3 0 8 6 6 9 2 *